Beowulf

Beowulf

*AN ADAPTATION BY JULIAN GLOVER
OF THE VERSE TRANSLATIONS OF
MICHAEL ALEXANDER AND EDWIN MORGAN*

JULIAN
GLOVER

SHEILA
MACKIE

MAGNUS
MAGNUSSON

ALAN SUTTON PUBLISHING LIMITED

First published 1987

Alan Sutton Publishing
Phoenix Mill · Far Thrupp · Stroud · Gloucestershire · GL5 2BU

First paperback edition 1995

British Library Cataloguing in Publication Data

[Beowulf. English] Beowulf.
I. Glover, Julian
829'.3   PR1583

ISBN 0-7509-1104-2

Designed by Martin Latham.
Typesetting by
Alan Sutton Publishing Limited.
Colour reproduction by
Spa Graphics Limited, Cheltenham.
Printed in Hong Kong by
Midas Printing Limited.

To Bruce Allsopp who also admires the Anglo Saxons and without whose invaluable help and support this book would not have been possible

SHEILA G. MACKIE

Contents

Foreword

Foreword

JULIAN GLOVER

I am an actor, who decided a few years ago, because of the irregularity of employment in my honourable but precarious profession, to attempt a 'One-Man Show'. A show that could be done anywhere at any time, without set or props, costumes or stage-manager, something that I could drop into at any convenient moment. Inspired by a suggestion from my wife, the actress Isla Blair, I put together a piece about the character and personality of the poet Robert Graves, who had been a close friend of my family for many years. I performed this show over about four years in many contrasting venues all over the British Isles, recorded it for television, and put it to rest after what I felt must be its Final Performance, in Robert's home village of Deya, in Mallorca.

I then began to look for a replacement. I was baulked in my search by the spectre of the

magnificent presentation by that fine actor Alec McCowan of, 'The Gospel According to St. Mark' – now known in theatrical circles as 'Alec's Gospel'! Baulked because, frankly, who could follow that? What material of a similar status could one perform without seeming to be climbing onto a band waggon? Obviously the other Gospels were unusable in this context and what, after all, could compete with The Greatest Story Ever Told?

So, I stopped 'looking' and instead I waited. I felt that looking would, for pragmatic reasons, produce a piece that would 'do' but, because of a lack of a fully centred commitment the final product would possibly be acceptable but unsatisfactory. I kept eyes and ears open of course, and considered many subjects, but nothing really caught my imagination and *told* me to do it.

That is, until one night in 1979 when, in the early hours, I woke suddenly with the memory of a story my mother had told me when I was small. I could recall only the names of the two main protagonists, Beowulf and Grendel (a name that even in that distant memory produced goose pimples) – nothing more. Next morning I almost ran to the Hammersmith Public Library and took out the first of the

many versions displayed there to catch my eye. I had only to read the first few lines to know that this was The One. I promptly bought Michael Alexander's *Penguin Classic* edition, which although I didn't realize it then, is by far the best, and started work that very day, producing my final version eighteen months later.

When I had read the whole poem (I was entranced to find it written in poetic form!), I realised that it was far too long to reproduce in its entirety over a single evening. My experience of the recital situation, both as listener and performer, has long convinced me that the patience and concentration of an audience should never be stretched beyond one and three-quarter hours, *with interval.* **Beowulf**, with its 3,182 lines would probably stretch to at least three and a half. But such is the nature of the method employed by the author (authors?) that the solution to the problem was immediately apparent. So clear in fact that it seemed almost as if it were 'meant'.

The story of Beowulf, Grendel, Grendel's mother and the Dragon, surely the basic story of all literature, is, in the original, approximately as long as the version offered here. There are, though, a very few cuts, made in order to keep

to the length I thought acceptable to a modern audience comparatively unused to the story-telling tradition. But the main excisions consist of stories unrelated to the central theme, stories of other kings, other peoples, other battles. I am convinced that these were gradually slipped in 'on demand' as the Scop — Story Teller — proceeded, and became diversions to draw out the experience and stretch the tension surrounding the 'big moments'. Tales recounted round the mead-hall fires of the eighth century would have spread over several days of wassail, with frequent interruptions for more food and drink, or sleep even, to be revived by requests for particular favourite historical or legendary anecdotes to eke out the whole. And this is what we have so fortunately inherited with the complete text known by the scholars as **Beowulf.**

My task, as I saw it, was to tell the story of the definitive hero, the warrior Beowulf. I am not an Early Englishman, but one of the twentieth century, and the test of the tale would be in succeeding to convey the excitement and joy of it through my own enthusiasm to people of all ages brought up in a climate of sophisticated theatre, film and television; to return to the

child at the knee, to enable an audience to experience a story as they did as children, providing through their own imaginations the setting, costumes and props. I hope that I have managed this with my performances around the world in such diverse venues as a Newcastle bookshop, St Cecilia's Hall, Edinburgh, the parish church of Upottery, the Pierrepoint Library, New York and the Khan Theatre, Jerusalem. If I have, it is further proof, if proof were needed after a thousand years, that **Beowulf** is a story for all time, for all races and cultures, and will never be irrelevant.

The two main sources of inspiration for this adaptation were the above-mentioned Penguin edition, and that of the poet Edwin Morgan. I also used a very short section from another Old English poem, *The Wanderer*, which I leave to the scholars to spot! To these, to Dr Malcolm Godden of Exeter College, Oxford and that fine actor, Michael Cronin, who both helped me so extensively, I extend my thanks for the insertions of Old English and many beautiful phrases and alliterations. And to the Great Guru, the definitive **Beowulf** critic, Klaeber, I acknowledge everlasting gratitude and admiration.

As far as I can see, all literature concerns, in

infinite variety of form, the Good Guy, Bad Guy conflict. The writers of **Beowulf** were simply the first to write it down. All commentaries on this extraordinary piece stress that it should be spoken out loud to evoke its full resonances. So, to the accompaniment of Sheila's magnificent illuminations, I suggest you try it. The rewards, as I know, are greater than may be imagined.

Waes Hael! Julian Glover

The first performance of Julian Glover's **Beowulf** *was given at the Theatre Room, Bretforton Grange on 5 September 1981, and was premiered in London at the Lyric Theatre Hammersmith in July of the following year.*

Introduction

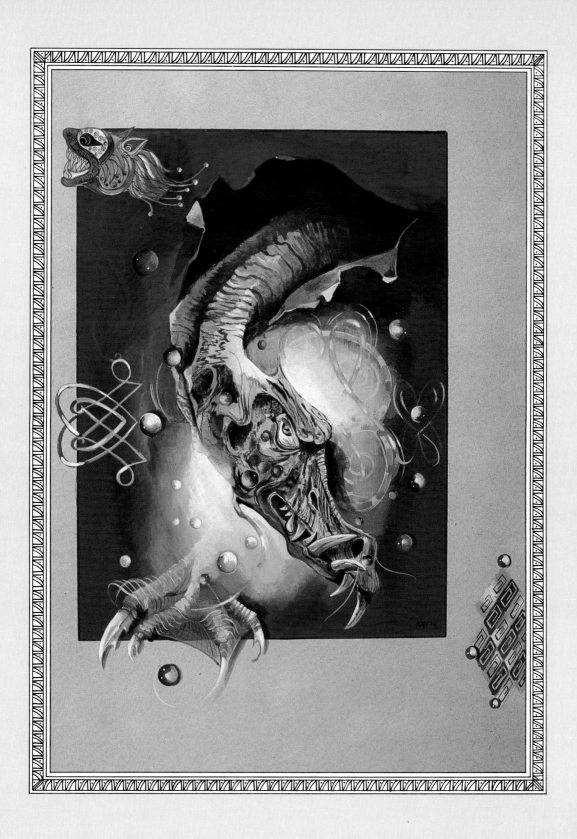

Introduction

MAGNUS MAGNUSSON

The stage is practically empty: a trestle table and a couple of benches draped with sheepskin rugs; an earthenware flagon, for wine; and a stout chair, centre stage, to represent a throne, with a ceremonial sword lying across it to symbolise royalty and power. Nothing else. Only a minimum of lighting effects.

Enter Julian Glover, to recount in resonant words one of the mightiest epic tales in world literature: the story of the great hero, **Beowulf** – Beowulf, slayer of dragons and defender of lands.

This is the two hours' traffic on the stage that Julian Glover presents: a man alone, like Beowulf himself, pitting himself against a formidable challenge. **Beowulf** is a heroic undertaking in every aspect, a one-man show *par excellence* that recreates with the authority of words and presence alone the sweep and

surging drive of a mighty narrative: heroic in concept, heroic in stature, heroic in utterance, heroic in achievement. It is an epic occasion that summons up a world whose trappings have long since disappeared, the trappings of the warrior ethos and morality of almost prehistoric Germanic times; but the essential 'message' has not changed. It is about courage and resolve, about duty and responsibility, about honour and achievement; but it is also about the transitoriness of things, the inevitability of death however glorious the life. It is both a celebration of humanity and an elegy. Through Julian Glover's commanding performance, it is also an unforgettable evening of theatre: this, surely, is how it must have been in days of old, when warriors sat at the ale-horns and heard the bards expound great stories of bygone days.

The poem, **Beowulf,** is one of the glories of European literature. It was composed in Old English (Anglo-Saxon) verse early in the 8th century, as far as we can tell, in the heyday of Anglian culture, probably in the Northumbria of the Venerable Bede and the Lindisfarne Gospels; but the oral material which informed it – the building-blocks of the epic, as it were – date back to the 6th century. It has come down

to us in only one surviving manuscript, which was made around the year 1000 and is now in the British Museum. In other circumstances it would be hailed as England's national epic, like the **Kalevala** of Finland; and certainly it dates from the very dawn of what can fairly be called English literature. Yet the poem, although composed in England, is not about England at all; it is set in the Scandinavian homelands from which the invading Angles and Saxons (the 'English' of the future) had come, bringing with them a rich heritage of ancestral Germanic legends and traditions.

These traditions were grounded in memories of a quasi-historical past – the past of the Danes and the Geats, a tribe who lived in the southern part of Sweden. In no sense can **Beowulf** be considered 'historical'; but there is one event in it that is frequently referred to and which serves to place the poem in the largely uncharted realm of legend. We know from a near contemporary source that one of the royal characters in **Beowulf,** the hero's liege lord Hygelac, king of the Geats, was killed in a raid on the Franks and the Frisians around the year 520. But Beowulf himself is pure legend. He did not live in any history that we know, nor did he belong to any

dynasty that we know. The historical framework is invoked merely to provide a recognisable context in which the hero operates.

Beowulf is a complex and intensely profound poem; but the story itself is relatively simple and straightforward. It is the story of a hero in action, presented in a series of significant incidents from his youth to his old age. These events are linked by the poet in a narrative of extreme discursiveness, full of allusions both to the past and to the known future, and introducing a number of subsidiary characters and supporting incidents. The archetypal Germanic society depicted in the poem, although familiar, is an idealised one, designed to highlight the mutual obligations of lord and liegeman of which Beowulf is an exemplary illustration. In this society, Beowulf stands out as being suprahuman: he has the strength of thirty men, he is able to swim under water for many hours at a time. Yet he has no attributes of divinity; when facing the powers of evil, the monsters which threaten the stability and order of human society, it is as a man, not a demi-god – but a man who is none the less cast in the almost religious role of a deliverer. Although the poem is set in the pre-Christian society of the Norse

lands, it was composed in the sophisticated Christian court-society of Anglian England, and the concept of God is explicitly present throughout in the poet's commentary on the action.

Beowulf opens with a celebration of the story of Scyld, the eponymous founder of the Scylding dynasty of the Danes, who came to Denmark alone over the sea as a helpless child and lived to found a great warrior empire. After a long and glorious reign he was returned to the sea in a ship-burial of unparalleled splendour – a scene that adumbrates the death and burial of Beowulf himself in the closing passages of the poem. The story passes on quickly to the time of Scyld's great-grandson, Hrothgar, a renowned and victorious king. To celebrate the success and prosperity of his reign, Hrothgar determined to build a mighty hall, the greatest mead-hall of all time; and he named it *Heorot* (the hall of the stag).

But Hrothgar was not able to enjoy Heorot long with his people. In the dank and misty fenland near the royal hall there lurked an evil monster called Grendel. He could not endure the sounds of merriment from within the hall, the music of the harp and the singing of mins-

trels telling the story of the Lord's Creation and the fiendish progeny of Cain that had been cast out from mankind. One night, enraged by the serene challenge of Heorot, the creature descended upon the hall and burst into it. The King's thanes were all blissfully asleep after an evening's carousing. Grendel seized thirty of them and carried them off to the lair in which he lived with his mother, a creature even more monstrous than himself. On the following night he returned, to commit further outrages; and from then on, no one dared to sleep in Heorot.

For twelve long years Heorot lay empty and abandoned at night, a gaunt symbol of the curse that had blighted Hrothgar's realm. No warrior, however brave, could defeat the creature in battle; no plan sufficed; no sacrifice to the ancient gods availed. Grendel ruled supreme.

Now word of the plight of the Danes reached the kingdom of the Geats; and there one of King Hygelac's warriors, his kinsman Beowulf, resolved to go to their assistance. He was a young man endowed with awesome strength of body, and was already renowned far and wide for his exploits. With a band of fourteen stout-hearted companions he set sail for Denmark. They landed on the rocky foreshore below the

ramparts of Heorot. A coast-warden saw their
arrival, this hard-knit group of warriors from
the sea, and challenged them gravely. Beowulf
declared the purpose of his mission to Heorot,
and he and his men were courteously ushered
into Hrothgar's presence.

The sea-journey and the arrival scene is a
brilliant *tour-de-force* of poetic description, and
it sets the stage superbly for the events that
follow. Beowulf stepped forward and offered
his services to Hrothgar: he requested the
honour of purging Heorot by fighting the
monster, unarmed, in single combat. Gratefully,
Hrothgar accepted; and for the first time in
twelve years the tables of Heorot were set for
feasting, and the rafters rang with music and
laughter. Only one jarring note was heard,
when an envious courtier called Unferth tried to
belittle one of Beowulf's earlier exploits – a
swimming-match against a companion named
Breca. For seven days they had swum in the
open sea in winter, and Breca had beaten
Beowulf – or so Unferth said. Beowulf replied
with barely restrained anger, and told what had
really happened: Breca and he had entered the
sea, each carrying a naked sword with which to
ward off whales. For five days and nights they

had stayed together, neither able to out-do the other, until the current separated them. Now sea-monsters moved in on the attack. One of them seized Beowulf and dragged him down to the depths of the ocean; but Beowulf's armour was impervious to its teeth, and with his sword he despatched the creature and several more. Far from losing the swimming-contest with Breca, Beowulf had emerged triumphant; and the nature of his victory boded well for the coming contest against the monstrous Grendel.

At nightfall, Hrothgar and his Danish warriors departed from the hall, to seek safety in bed elsewhere, leaving Beowulf and his Geats on guard. Beowulf took off his helmet and armour and lay down to rest. His companions also laid down their weary limbs, and quickly fell asleep.

Through the darkness of the night came Grendel, drawn to the hall by the unwonted sounds of feasting. In a flash he tore down the doors and seized hold of the first sleeping warrior he saw, ripped him apart and bolted him down. But as he reached out for another victim, he felt his arm grasped in a grip more powerful than he had ever met before: Beowulf had stayed awake, and now caught him in an

unbreakable hold. The great hall shuddered as the combatants lunged to and fro. And now Gredel realised that he had met more than his match at last. Desperately he tried to escape from the struggle, but he only managed to get away from Beowulf's terrible grip when his arm was torn from his shoulder. Grendel fled the hall, mortally injured, to seek refuge in his lair in the fens.

Beowulf had now fulfilled his promise. When the Danes returned to the hall in the morning, they saw Grendel's arm hanging from the rafters as proof of victory. Many of the warriors took horse and followed the bloodstained trail that Grendel had left as he staggered homewards, and looked in wonder at the boiling, bloodied waters of the mere in which he had made his lair. Hrothgar showered gifts on Beowulf, and took him to his bosom as if he were his own son. Once again the great hall of Heorot resounded with rejoicing, while minstrels gladdened men's hearts with tales of heroism and battle. When the banquet was over, Hrothgar and Beowulf and his Geat companions left the hall, which was left in the keeping of a host of Danish warriors.

But the rejoicing was premature. There had

for long been a widespread rumour that there were two monsters, not one – that Grendel had had a dam who was still alive. And that very night, Grendel's mother, grieving over the loss of her son, emerged from the lair in the mere, grimly resolved on vengeance for her offspring.

At this point the stage performance pauses for the Interval. There is a feeling of almost stunned pleasure amongst the audience: **Beowulf** had never been like this when we struggled through it at University with our Anglo-Saxon primers. Julian Glover has brought out all the dramatic sweep and surge of the narrative, reminding us what a great work of art it is when read and presented by an artist. But the story is by no means done. . . .

The second half of the performance opens as Grendel's mother found the Danish warriors asleep in Heorot. She seized hold of one of the king's favourite champions and made off with him to the fens, after snatching Grendel's arm down from the rafters.

It was now time for Beowulf to prove himself again. With a company of Danes and Geats he went to the lake where the monsters had their underwater lair. There Beowulf donned his armour, and accepted from the craven Unferth a

celebrated sword called Hrunting. And with
that he plunged into the lake. It took him until
noon to reach the bottom of the lake, where
Grendel's mother sprang at him and dragged
him into her lair. Beowulf's armour saved him
from hurt; but when he struck at the monster
with the sword Hrunting, the sword failed to
bite. After a titanic struggle, Beowulf managed
to get hold of an ancient giant sword that hung
from the wall, and with that he killed Grendel's
mother.

The onlookers on the banks of the lake had
seen the waters boil furiously and grow red with
blood. By the middle of the afternoon they felt
sure that Beowulf was dead, and King Hrothgar
and his Danish warriors sorrowfully returned
home. Only Beowulf's companions were left —
and they feared the worst. But Beowulf had
survived, and when he reached the surface at last
he was given a rapturous welcome by his men,
and later at Heorot.

Next morning, Beowulf and his Geats depart-
ed for their homeland, their mission accom-
plished. Beowulf dutifully gave to his lord,
Hygelac, the treasures he had been given in
Denmark, and received gifts in return. Later,
when Hygelac was killed during the raid on the

Franks and the Frisians around the year 520, Beowulf loyally supported his son Heardred. It was not until Heardred himself died in a war against the Swedes that Beowulf became ruler of the kingdom of the Geats. For fifty years he ruled it, 'growing grey in guardianship of the land'. But there was one more test of his manhood, his heroic virtue as the defender of his people, for Beowulf to undergo.

It so happened that there was a hoard of gold in a burial mound, which was jealously guarded by a dragon. This dragon had lain there for three centuries without doing anyone harm, until one day a runaway slave found his way into the burial mound and stole a gold cup to take back to his master as a peace offering. Enraged by the loss, the dragon started devastating the countryside, burning every building it could find, including Beowulf's hall.

Beowulf now prepared himself for what he surely knew would be his last great battle: once again the forces of evil had broken loose and were menacing the stability of the kingdom. With eleven companions he set out for the dragon's lair. Once again, he insisted on fighting the creature alone. But now his diminishing strength and his trusty weapons failed him. Soon

he was being overwhelmed by the flames of the dragon. At this crucial hour of his need, all his companions fled the scene, except for one faithful retainer, Wiglaf, a prince of the royal house of the Geats. Seeing his liege lord in deadly trouble, Wiglaf surged to his help. The dragon was distracted long enough for Beowulf to get in a blow with his sword; but the dragon pounced on Beowulf, and dealt him a terrible wound in the neck. Between them, Beowulf and Wiglaf managed to finish off the dragon; but Beowulf was now mortally wounded.

A great funeral pyre was built on a headland; and there the hero's body was consigned to the flames amongst his accoutrements of war and his personal treasures. Then a royal burial mound was erected over the site of the pyre, and the hero's personal treasures piled into the tomb. Twelve of his retainers rode round the mound in an ecstasy of lamentation.

> *This was the manner of the mourning*
>   *of the Geats,*
> *Sharers in the feast, at the fall of their lord;*
> *They said he had proved of all*
>   *kings in the world*
> *The gentlest of men, the most gracious,*

*The kindest to his people, the keenest
for fame.*

Beowulf, as presented by Julian Glover on
stage and reproduced in book form here, is not
the full poem as it has come down to us. It has
been reduced to something like half of its
original length, partly because of the fear that a
full four-hour presentation might over-tax our
modern limits of patience and concentration,
and partly because the poem contains so much
discursive matter that tends to blur the hard
cleanness of the story-line.

It translates readily to the stage, for it was
originally designed for public performance, to
be uttered aloud. It was composed in a trad-
itional oral style that had been developing and
evolving for a long time. For such public project-
ion, the sheer energy of the narrative, the
beauty of the sounds of the Anglo-Saxon verse,
the subtle rhythm and flow of the sentences, the
alliteration and assonances that held lines
together – all these were of paramount
importance.

That is why Julian Glover chose as the basis
of his theatre-script the verse translation by
Professor Michael Alexander (*Penguin Classics,*

1973). It is an admirable version that has caught, better than any other I know, the poetic power and eloquence of the original. Julian Glover has occasionally embellished Professor Alexander's text with borrowings from the poet Edwin Morgan, the distinguished doyen of literary critics and translators in Scotland, and has rearranged the material in places to suit the demands of dramatic production.

Sheila Mackie's illustrations to this book are a superb enhancement to the experience of **Beowulf**. Like the original diction of the poem, they might be called visual 'kennings': elaborate visual metaphors that enrich the texture of the vocabulary of the poetry. The word *kenning* is a technical term (it is derived from a verb meaning 'to teach') for the periphrastic descriptive compounds which abounded in Old English and Old Icelandic poetry; they were used to give familiar words a fresh charge of meaning by bringing out their pictorial and emotional colour. Thus, the idea of the sea is heightened by calling it the *swan-rad*, which literally means 'swan-riding', in the sense of the region in which the swan swims; the kenning evokes a sharp visual reminder in our minds of a natural aspect of the sea.

Similarly, a kenning for 'body' such as *ban-hus* ('bone-house') brings to mind the image of the body as a building timbered with beams and supports of bone. Even a stock phrase such as *woruld-candel* ('world-candle') for 'sun' can refresh a word grown ordinary with familiarity; and when a sword is described as *beado-leoma*, 'battle-light', we seem to see the bright blade flashing in the dusty din of battle.

In the same way, Sheila Mackie has created compound collages of symbols and images to counterpoint the story at particular points. She has carefully studied all the examples of material culture that have survived from Anglo-Saxon times — the swords and shields, the jewellery and art-work, the horse-trappings and the armour. Much of this material has come from the excavation of the celebrated ship-burial at Sutton Hoo in Suffolk, where some 7th century East Anglian ruler was laid to rest in full panoply, surrounded by his personal treasures.

These exact models have given her work a satisfying sense of realism: we can say with confidence, Yes, these are the sort of accoutrements that the author of **Beowulf** had in mind

when he was describing the events of the past. But some things are not made explicit in the poem. We are not told precisely what the monsters looked like; we are only given an impression of terror, an indication of dreadful size and strength, a nightmarish outline of ferocity and fire. The monsters of **Beowulf** are creatures that inhabit the hinterlands of our subconscious fears. It is here that the imagination of the artist speaks for us all in language that must be symbolic rather than naturalistic.

The style of her illustrations reinforces the idea of **Beowulf** as a literary pageant, a known and remembered background of Northern warrior dynasties with their demanding social *mores* and involved political alliances, against which the author manipulates combinations of stock figures and archetypal events to personalise the main theme of deliverance through heroic virtue. In this pageant, the central figure is the incarnation of the hero-ideal: a human being with access to superhuman attributes, but a human nonetheless. It is this highly stylised, symbolic background that Sheila Mackie has evoked so graphically, just as Julian Glover does on stage with such potent eloquence alone.

It is a visual style that ultimately harks back

to the artistry of the scribes who illustrated the handsome vellum or parchment manuscripts they penned. These illustrations, which often took the form of elaborate initial capitals at the start of a new chapter or section, were designed to highlight the matter of the manuscripts. They are called 'illuminations'; and illumination is precisely what Sheila Mackie has given the text in rich measure with her immensely effect-ive pictorial kennings.

Magnus Magnusson

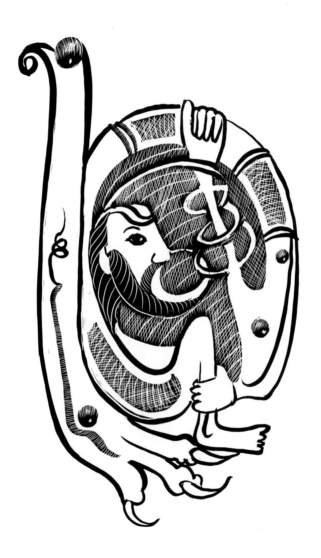

Beowulf

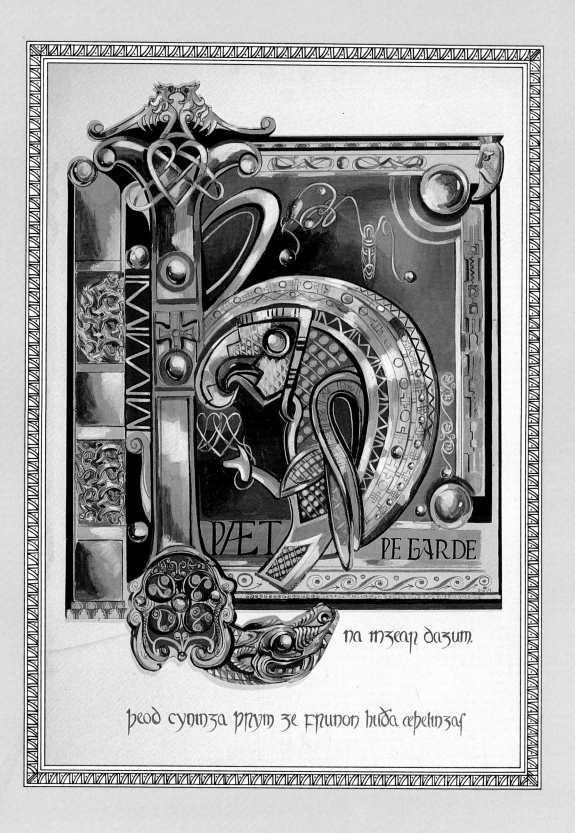

HÞÆT   ÞE ĠARDE

na inġear daġum.

þeod cyninġa þrym ġe frunon huða æþelinġaſ

hear-listen

We have heard of the thriving of the throne of Denmark,
How the folk-kings flourished in former days,
How those royal athelings earned that glory.

Was it not Scyld Sheving that shook the halls,
Took mead-benches, taught encroaching foes
    to fear him –
Who, found in childhood, lacked clothing?
Yet, he lived and prospered, grew in strength
    and stature under the heavens.
Ðæt wæs gōd cyning!   He was a good king!

A boy child was afterwards born to Scyld,
A young child in hall-yard, a hope for the people,

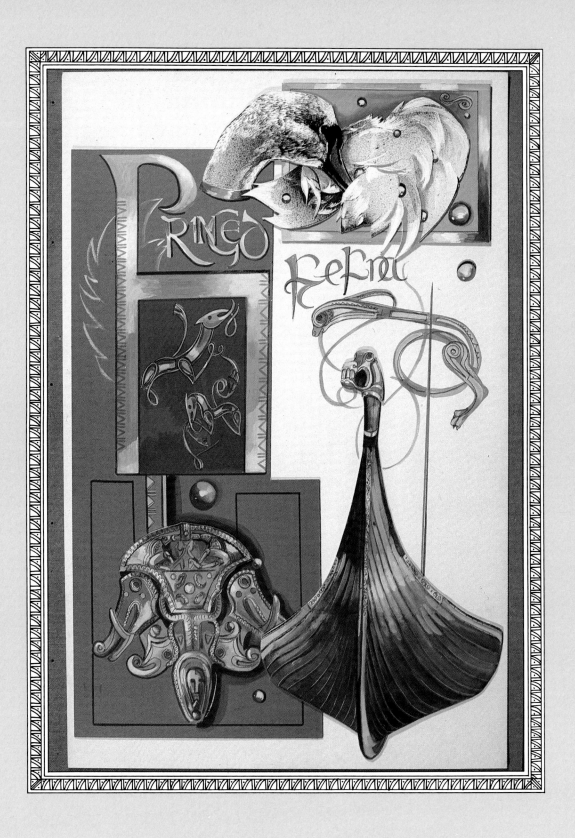

Sent them by God. The life-bestowing,
Wielder of Glory granted them this blessing and
Through the northern lands his name sprang widely.
For in youth an atheling should so use his virtue,
That in old age, when enemies gather,
Established friends should stand by him
And serve him gladly. It is by glorious action
That a man comes by honour in any people.

At the hour shaped for him, Scyld departed,
The hero crossed into the keeping of his Lord.
A boat with ringed neck rode in the haven,
Icy, out-eager, the atheling's vessel,
And there they laid out their lord and master,
Giver of wound gold, in the waist of the ship,
In majesty by the mast. A mound of treasures
From far countries was fetched aboard her,
And it is said that no boat was ever more bravely
  fitted out
With weapons of a warrior, war accoutrement,
Swords and body-armour.

High over head they hoisted and fixed
A gold signum; gave him to the flood,
Let the seas take him. Men under heaven's
Shifting skies, though skilled in counsel,
Cannot say surely where that freight was washed.

Then for a long space there lodged in the stronghold
Three generations, ending with King Hrothgar,
    Son of Healfdene.
And to this Hrothgar was granted glory in battle,
Mastery of the field; so friends and kinsmen
Gladly obeyed him, and his band grew
To a great company. It came into his mind
That he would command the construction
Of a huge mead-hall, a house greater
Than men on earth ever had heard of,
And share the gifts God had bestowed on him
Upon its floor with folk young and old.

Far and wide (as I heard it) the work was given out
In many a tribe over middle earth

For the making of the mead-hall, and, as men reckon,
The day of readiness dawned very soon
For this best of houses. He named it Heorot;
  'Hall of the Stag'.
He made good his boast, gave out rings and
Arm-bands at the banquet. Boldly the hall reared
Its arched gables. The time was not yet
When the blood-feud should bring out again
Sword-hatred in sworn kindred.

It was with pain that a powerful spirit,
Dwelling in darkness, endured that time,
Hearing daily the hall filled with loud amusement.
There was music of the harp, sweet minstrel singing,
Perfect in telling, of the remote first making
  of the race of man.
The minstrel told how, long ago, the Lord
  formed Earth.
Wlitebeorhtne wang, swā wæter bebūgeð,
Gesette sigehrēþig sunnan ond mōnan,
Lēoman tō lēohte landbūendum,

Ond gefrætwade foldan scēatas
Leomum ond lēafum, līf ēac gesceōp
Cynna gehwylcum þāra ðe cwice hwyrfaþ;
'A plain, bright to look on, locked in ocean;
Exulting, the Lord established the sun and
   the moon
As lamps to illumine the land-dwellers;
Loaded the acres of the world in the jewelwork
Of branch and leaf, bringing then to life
Each kind of creature that creeps and moves'.

So, the company of men led a careless life,
   all was well with them;
Till this one spirit, hell in his mind, his malice began.
Grendel, the fiend's name: grim, infamous
Wasteland stalker, master of the moor and the
   fen fortress.
This unhappy being had long lived in the land
   of the monsters
Since the Creator cast them out as kindred of Cain.

Far from mankind God drove out Cain for
    his deed of shame!
And from him came down all kinds of misbegotten,
Kobolds and gogmagogs, lemures and zombies,
And the brood of titans that battled with God
    ages long.
He gave them their reward.

With the coming of night came Grendel also.
He found in Heorot the nobles after carousing,
Slept after supper, far from the sorrows and
    the miseries of men.
Mad with rage, he struck quickly, this creature of evil:
Grim and greedy, savage and unsparing,
Grasped thirty warriors, and away he was homeward,
Glutlusty with booty, laden with the slain.
Hūðe hrēmig tō hām faran,
Mid þǣre wælfylle wīca nēosan.

When the day broke, and with the dawn's light
Grendel's outrage was openly to be seen:

Then weeping arose where feasting had been
Loud morning crying. Lord Hrothgar
Sat silent then, the strong man mourned,
Glorious king, he wept for his thanes
As they saw the footprints of the terrible foe,
  the cursed fiend.
Nor did he let them rest but the next night again
Brought new horrors, murder, manslaughter
  and outrage,
And shrank not from it.

It was not remarkable then if a man looked
For sleeping-quarters quieter, less central,
Among the outer buildings; now openly shown
The new hall-thane's hatred was manifest
  and unmistakable.
Each survivor then kept a safer distance.

So, Grendel became ruler. Empty then stood
That best of houses, and for no brief space,

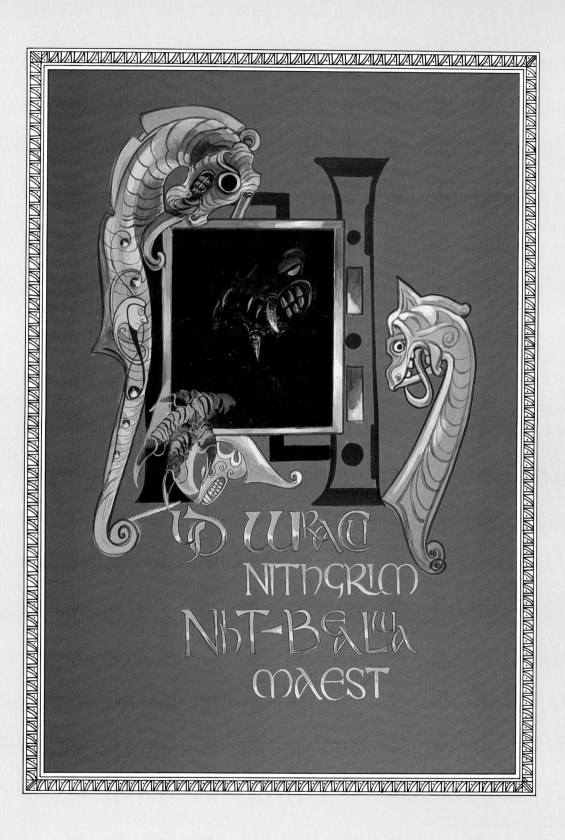

For twelve long winters torment sat
On the Lord of the Scyldings; songs were sung,
How Grendel warred on Hrothgar, the wrongs
   he did him.
How, abominable, he watched and waited for them,
   walked nightlong
The misty moorland. And what man's knowledge
Can map the gliding ground of demon and damned?

The council lords sat daily to devise some plan,
What might be best against these terror-raids,
Promising sometimes on the altars of their idols
Unholy sacrifices, if the Slayer of Souls
Would bring some relief to the suffering people.
Hell possessed their hearts and minds:
The Lord God was unknown to them,
   that Wielder of Glory.
This season rocked the son of Healfdene
With swingeing sorrows; too cruel the strife,
Too strong and long-lasting, night-frightfulness unequalled.
Nȳdwracu nīþgrim, nihtbealwa mǣst.

Part One

This Grendel feud was heard of by one of King
    Hygelac's warriors,
Brave among the Geats from over the seas.
He was for main strength of all men foremost
That trod the earth at that time;
Great framed, great heart. Æþele ond ēacen.
He had a seaworthy wave-cutter fitted out for him:
The warrior king Hrothgar he would seek, he said,
    over the swan's riding,
That lord of great name, desperate for men.
The prince picked his men from the flower of his folk,
The fiercest among them that might be found.
Fourteen;
Sea-skilled Beowulf led them down to the beach's
    fringe.

Time running on, the boat rode the waves hard
*   in by the headland.*
Harnessed warriors leaped on prow;
Surf was swirling, sand was stirring;
Bright mail-coats to the mast's foot were carried,
War-gear well-wrought; willingly they shoved her out,
Their tight timbered craft, on the craved voyage.
Away she went, over the wavy ocean,
Boat like a bird, breaking the seas,
Wind-whetted, white-throated,
Till the curved prow had ploughed so far
That after a space on only the second day
They might see land loom on the skyline,
The shimmer of cliffs, sheer fells behind,
*   ample promontories.*
The crossing was at an end.

The Geatish men stepped on strand, moved briskly up,
A rope going ashore, ring-mail clashed, battle-girdings –
A watchman saw them! From the wall where he stood,
Posted by the Scyldings to protect the cliffs,

He saw the polished shields pass along the gangway,
And curiosity moved him to know who these men were.
This thane, when his horse had picked its way
down to the shore, shook his spear fiercely
At arm's length, framed the challenge:
'Strangers, you have steered this steep craft
Through the sea-ways, and sought out our coast.
I see you are warriors;
I must ask who you are. In all my years
I have lived as look-out at land's end here
Shield-carriers have never come ashore more openly.
You had no word of leave from the great King
    Hrothgar!
I have not in my life set eyes on a man
With more might in his frame than this helmed lord.
He's no hall-fellow, no mere retainer tricked out
    in armour,
Unless looks belie him; he has the head of a hero.
I'll have your names now and the names of your fathers,
Or further you shall not go — stay where you
    are strangers!
Say where you are from, why you are come.'

The captain gave him a clear answer: 'We here
   are come from the country of the Geats,
And are hearth-companions to the great King
   Hygelac.
My noble father was known as Edgetheow,
Fighter famous 'mong nations: all wiser men
In the world remember him readily.
It is with loyal and true intention that we come
To seek your lord, the son of Healfdene.
We have a great errand to that glorious hero
Shepherd of the Danes: the drift of it
Shall not be kept from you. You must know,
   if indeed
There is truth in what is told in our country
   Geatland,
That among you Scyldings some strange enemy,
An obscure assaillant in the opaque night-times,
Makes spectacles of spoil and slaughter in hideous
   feud.
To Hrothgar I would openheartedly unfold a plan
How that old commander may overcome his foe;
If indeed an easing is ever to slacken

EOFOR-LIC

scionon ofer hlor - bergan gehroden golde fah
onð fyr - heard ferh - weardeheold
guþmodgum men

These besetting sorrows:
Otherwise he must miserably live out this
 lamentable time
For as long as Heorot, hall of halls, bulks to the sky.'

The mounted coastguard made reply: 'I accept
 what I am told, that this troop is loyal
To the Scyldings' Protector. Pass forward,
 I'll guide you:
Commanding meanwhile the men under me
To guard with care this craft of yours,
This ship on the sand fresh from its tarring,
Till again it bear its beloved captain
With curve-necked keel to the coast of Geat.'

The vessel was still as they set forward,
The deep-chested ship stayed at its mooring
Fast at its anchor.
Briskly the men went marching together,
Each helmet sparkling with glancing boar-emblems,
Patterned and fire tempered, brilliant with gold,

Till they made out at last the home of the king:
The most illustrious hall under heaven
Its radiance lighting the lands of the world.
Their guide pointed up to the shining palace,
Then brought his horse round and said
   in the quiet: 'Here I must leave you.
May the Lord Almighty
Afford you His grace in your great undertaking
And bring you in safety back to the sea-shore.'

The path that brought the band on its way
   was paved with stone.

Their war-coats shone as they marched along
In their gear of grim aspect going to the hall.
Sea-wearied, they then set against the wall
   their polished shields.
The weapons of the seamen stood in a spear-rack,
An ash-wood, grey-tipped. These iron shirted men
Were handsomely armed. A nobleman there,
   Wulfgar, said, 'I am spokesman here,
   herald to Hrothgar.

It is not exile but adventure I am thinking
That brings you to Heorot.
From whence do you bring
These embellished shields, grey war-coats,
  masked helmets
This stack of spears?' The gallant Geat
  gave answer then,
Wlanc Wedera lēod, word æfter spræc
Valour-renowned, hard under helmet:
'At Hygelac's table we are sharers in the feast:
Beowulf is my name; I shall set out to Hrothgar
The cause of my journey, so tell him.'
Then Wulfgar replied: 'The Lord of the Danes,
Protector of the Scyldings, shall learn of your
  request.
I shall willingly ask my honoured chief,
Giver of rings, of your undertaking,
And soon bear the answer back my lord shall
  think to make.'
He rapidly strode to the seat of Hrothgar:
  'Men have come here from the country of Geatland,
Borne from afar on the back of the sea:

These battle-companions call the man who leads them,
   Beowulf.
Do not, kind Hrothgar, refuse them audience;
Their accoutrement clearly bespeaks them of
   earl's rank,
And their leader seems to command them by right.'

The Guardian of the Scyldings gave his answer:
   'Him? I knew him when he was a child!
His old father, Edgetheow and I fought together.
   Well does the son
Now pay this call on a tested friend.
The seafarers used to say, I remember,
That this fighting man in his hand's grasp had
   the strength
Of thirty other men. I believe the Lord God
Has directed him here against Grendel's oppression.
Waste no time now but tell them to come in.'

Promptly Wulfgar, in rite of decorum,
Turned to the door and told his message:

'The Master of Battles, Lord of the North Danes,
Bids me to announce, that he knows your ancestry.
I am to tell you, determined warriors,
You may go in now in your gear of battle,
Set eyes on Hrothgar, helmed as you are.'

Then Beowulf arose, surrounded by his soldiers,
The Geats swung in across Heorot's floor.
Thick-thronging retinue, the warrior leading,
Helmeted, grave, till he stopped at the hearth.
'Wæs þū, Hrōðgār, hāl!
'I am Hygelac's kinsman and serve in his fellowship.
Word of Grendel has been made known to me.
The sailors speak of this hall standing idle, silent
    of voices,
As soon as the evening's light has hid 'neath
    heaven's hood.
I'm urged by my counsellors to seek you
    sovereign Hrothgar.
These men know well the weight of my hands.
Have they not seen me come home from fights

Where I have bound five Giants, or crushed
  on the waves
Sea-serpents by night and broken the beasts?
And shall I not try a single match,
A trial against this fiend, this monster Grendel?
I have now therefore to make you this request,
To ask one sole favour, Protector of the Scyldings;
Not to forbid me, with my loyal companions,
To cleanse your hall Heorot, having come this far!
As I am informed that this unlovely one
Is careless enough to carry no weapon,
I abjure utterly the bearing of sword.
With naked hands shall I grapple with the fiend,
Fight to the death here, hater and hated!
He who is chosen shall give himself to God.
If he can contrive it we may count upon Grendel
To eat quite fearlessly the flesh of we Geats
Here in this war-hall. There will be no need, Sir,
For you to bury my head; he will have it gladly.
He will bear my corpse away, bent on eating it.
Bespatter his moor-lair, without another thought.
But if the fight should take me, I ask you

send King Hygelac
This best of battle-shirts which my breast now wears.
It is the queen of war coats and from the forge
 of Wayland.
Fate- Wyrd *-will take its course.'*
*G*æ*ð* ā *wyrd swā h*ī*o scel.* '

Then Hrothgar spoke, the helmet of the Scyldings:
 'So it is to fight in our defence friend Beowulf,
And as an office of kindness that you come to us here!
It is a sorrow in spirit for me to say to any man
What the hatred of Grendel has brought us to in Heorot.
My hall-companions, my war-band are dwindled,
Doom-swept away by Grendel and horror.
They often boasted, when the beer was drunk,
That they would here await, in this wassailing-place
With daunting blade for Grendel's assault.
But each time the morning brought light of day
This mead-hall was seen all stained with blood:
Blood had soaked its shining floor, it was a
 house of slaughter.

Yet sit now to the banquet, should the mood
*   so take you.'*

A bench was then cleared for the company of Geats
There in the beer-hall, for the whole band together.
Prompt in his office, the man who held the mead horn
Poured out its sweetness. The song of the poet
Again rang in Heorot. The heroes laughed loud
The Geats and Danes together.

Then Unferth spoke, one of Hrothgar's warriors,
Sitting at the feet of the Father of the Scyldings.
He could not allow that any other name
Should hold a higher title than went with his own.
* 'Is this the Beowulf of Breca's swimming match,*
When for pride the pair of you tested the seas,
And for a trite oath entrusted your lives
To the deep waters. A sorry contest!
Your arms embraced the ocean's streams,
You beat the wave-way, wove your hand-movements,
The sea boiled with waves of winter:

You laboured seven nights; and then you lost!
His might was the greater; daylight found him
Cast by the sea on the coast of Norway.
He made his way home did Breca son of Beanstan,
Performed to the letter what he promised to you.
I see little hope then of happier outcome –
Though in other conflicts elsewhere in the world
You may indeed have prospered – if you intend keeping
Your all night vigil in Grendel's path.'

Then Beowulf spoke, son of Edgetheow: 'I thank
    my friend Unferth, who unlocks us this tale
Of Breca's bragged exploit; the beer in his gut
    lends
Eloquence to his tongue. But as for the truth;
I had more sea-strength and endured underwater
    worse struggle than he.
It was something the two of us said as boys,
Boasting how we should venture our lives on the ocean,
Which in due time we accordingly did.
Hard in our right hands we each held a sword

As we went through the seas,
So to defend ourselves 'gainst whale and killer.
He could not away from me, nor would I from him.
Thus, stroke for stroke we stitched the ocean
Five nights and days, when a current split us,
A churning of waters in chilliest of weathers.
Blackness lowering, north wind bending
Hostile against us: the waves were rough!
The unfriendliness was then aroused of the fishes
    of the deep.
Against these beasts my body-armour helped me,
This forge-knit battleshirt bright with gold.
Then a savage attacker dragged me to the bottom,
Pinned me in his grip. But I got the chance
To stab the ugly creature with my weapon's point.
Then more loathsome snouts snickered by me,
    swarmed at my throat.
But those scaly flesh-eaters sat not down to dine
    on Beowulf.
They picniced not on me. Daylight found them,
Mauled by my sword, up along the beaches,
Soundly asleep, since when they have never

Troubled any traveller over that deep-water-way.
Day in the east grew, the billows sank,
So I then could see the headlands, the windy cliffs.
I came with my life from the compass of my foes,
But tired from the struggle. Wyrd oft nereð
Unfægne eorl, þonne his ellen dēah!
Aye, fate is often merciful to the brave man.
And it was my part to put to the sword
    seven sea-monsters;
A man more sorely pressed the seas never held.
No whisper has yet reached me
Of sword-ambushes survived nor such scathing perils
In connection with your name! Never has Breca
Nor you Unferth either, in open battle-play
Framed such a deed with your shining swords.
I tell you, Unferth,
This Grendel had never grown such a terror,
This demon had never dealt your lord
Such havoc in Heorot had your heart's intention
Been so grim for battle as you give us to believe.
He's learnt there's no need to fear your people.
He spares not a single sprig of you Danes

In extorting his tribute, and expects no resistance
From the spear-wielding Scyldings. I'll show him Geatish
Strength and stubborness shortly enough now,
A lesson in war.
He who wishes shall then go blithe to the banquet
When the flame-mailed sun of another day
Shall dawn for men in the southern sky.'

Then was laughter of heroes, harp-music ran,
Words were warm-hearted. Wealhtheow, the queen
  of Hrothgar,
Moved forward, mindful of courtesies,
Glittering, to welcome the Geats in the hall,
Peerless lady; but to the land's guardian
She offered first the flowing cup,
Then the old and the young men in each part
  of the hall
Until the time came when the flashing-armed queen
Carried to Beowulf the brimming vessel;
She spoke to him kindly, gave thanks to Lord God
In words wisely chosen, her wish being granted

To meet with a man who might be relied on
For aid against these troubles.

Then up spoke Beowulf son of Edgetheow:
'This was my determination in taking to the ocean,
That I should once and for all accomplish the wishes
Of your adopted people. I shall achieve victory
Or here in this mead-hall meet my ending day!'
This speech sounded sweet to the glittering lady.

Then was King Hrothgar minded to rest,
Aware of the monster brooding his attack
From the time when he saw the sun's first light
To the time when darkness drowns all things.
And under its shadow-cover shapes do glide
Dark beneath the clouds. The whole assembly rose up.
Then did the King with these words leave Beowulf:
    'Never have I at any instance to any man
Thus handed over Heorot as I here do to you.
    Take, and now hold to the house of the Danes!
Bend your mind and your body, and wake
    against the foe!'

Beowulf then replied with a boasting speech:
  'I fancy my fighting-strength, my performance in
    combat
At least as greatly as Grendel does his:
And therefore, I shall not foreshorten his life
With a slashing sword – too simple a business.
Of good arms he knows nothing, of the shattering
  of shields.
No, we'll at night play without any weapons –
If unweaponed he dare to face me in fight.
The Father in His wisdom shall apportion the
  honours then,
The All-holy Lord to whichever he think fit.'
Then the hero lay down, while about him many
Brave sea-warriors bent to their hall-rest.
Not one of them thinking ever to see again
Their beloved country.

Cōm on wanre niht scrīðan sceadugenga.
Gliding through the shadows came the
    walker in the night.
The warriors slept — all except one,
And this man kept an unblinking watch.
He waited, pent-heart swelling with anger 'gainst
    his foe.
From off the moorlands' misting fells
    Came Grendel stalking.
Ðā cōm of mōre under misthleoþum
    Grendel gongan.
He moved through the dark, saw with perfect clearness
The gold panelled hall, mead-drinking place of men.
The door gave way at a touch of his hands.
Rage-inflamed, wreckage-bent, he tore the hall's jaws.
Hastening onwards, angrily advancing,
From his eyes shot a light in unlovely form of fire.
He saw in the hall the host of young warriors
And in his heart exulted, horrible monster,
All his hopes swelling to a gluttonous meal.
He meant to divide, monstrous in frightfulness,
The life from each body that lay in that place.

As a first step he set his greedy hands on
A sleeping soldier, savagely tore him,
Gnashed at his bone-joints, bolted huge gobbets,
Sucked at his veins, and had soon eaten
All of the man, to his fingers and feet.
Then he moved forward, reached to seize our
     warrior Beowulf,
Stretched out for him with his spite filled fist:
But the faster man forestalling, rose up upon his arm
And quickly gripped that sickening hand.
The upholder of evils immediately knew
He had not met on middle earth's acres
With any other man of a harder hand-grasp.
He strained to be off, he ailed for his darkness,
His company of devils and his den beneath the mere;
But Hygelac's brave Kinsman recalled his
     evening's utterance
And tightened his hold till fingers burst.
The monster strained away; the man stepped closer;
The monster's desire was for darkness between them,
Direction regardless, to get out and run

For *his fen-bordered lair. It was an ill journey*
That persecutor had of it when he made for Heorot.

It was indeed wonderful that the wine-supper hall
Withstood the wrestling pair, that the world's great
   palace
Fell not to the ground. But it was girt firmly,
Both inside and out, with iron braces
Of skilled manufacture. Many a
Gold-worked wine-bench, as we heard it,
Started from the floor at the struggles of that pair.
A thing undreamed of by Scylding wisdom
Was that any of mankind by what method soever
Might undo that intricate antlered hall,
Sunder it by strength – unless it were swallowed in
   embraces of fire.

Fear entered the Danes as they heard through
   the side-wall
The grisly plaint of the enemy of God,

The sobs of the damned one bewailing his pain.
The Geats leapt up to defend their great prince:
They were ignorant then that no sword on earth
Not the truest of steel could touch their assaillant,
For every sword-edge and weapon of victory
* he had blunted by wizardry.*

It was then that this monster, moved by spite
* 'gainst our race,*
Found in the end flesh and bone were to fail him;
For Hygelac's great kinsman, stout-hearted warrior,
Had him fast by the hand; and hateful to each
Was the breath of the other.
A rip in the giant flesh-frame showed then,
Shoulder-muscles sprang apart, a snapping of
Tendons, bone-locks burst;
The arm of the demon was severed from his side,
And Grendel flew, death sick, to his joyless den
Where he knew that the end of his life was in sight.
Beowulf had cleansed Heorot, saved the hall
* from persecution.*

As a signal to all the hero hung the hand,
The arm and torn-off shoulder, the entire limb,
Grendel's whole grip, beneath the soaring roof.

Then it was as I heard it, at hall next morning,
Warrior with warrior walked to see this ghastly limb.
The Athelings gazed at the hand, high under ceiling:
Each nail-socket seemed steel to the eye,
Each spur on the hand was a talon of fear.
Of the bright building just the roof had survived
Unmarred and in one piece.
Along the wide highroads the chiefs of the clans came
Crossed remote tracts to follow the foe's footprints,
Who with strength flagging
Had staggered to his fen-lair giving up his heathen soul.
There, the death-daubed waters,
    Becrimsoned, seethed, gore-hot,
And hell engulfed his life in the deep fen pool.
Then the clan chiefs wheeled away from the mere
    in bold mood
Joined by the young men, white-mounted warriors.

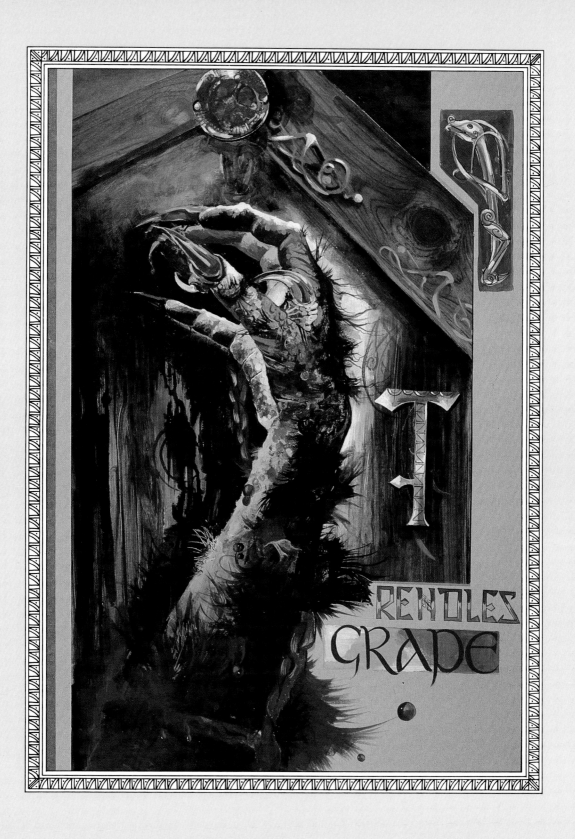

Of Beowulf many said that over earth's stretch
Of all who wielded sword he was worthiest to rule.
(In saying this they did not slight in the least
The gracious Hrothgar, for he was a good king.)
    Ac þæt wæs gōd cyning.

Taking his stand on the steps of the hall,
Hrothgar beheld the hand of Grendel, said:
    'Beowulf, I now take you to my bosom as a son.
Hold yourself well in this new relation!
You will lack nothing that lies in my gift.
May the Almighty Father yield you always the success
That on your own account you have guaranteed
    in deeds.'

Then Beowulf spoke, son of Edgetheow: 'I had
    meant to catch him, clamp him with a lock-hold,
And I clung to him too loosely to prevent his escape.
But now he lives no longer, is forced to await
Till the Lord in His splendour shall pass his
    great decree.'

Then, as a sign of victory, Hrothgar, Son of Healfdene
Presented to Beowulf a sword worked in gold.
And onto the floor had brought on eight war-horses
With glancing bridles, one with a saddle
Studded with stones – battle seat of the Danes.
He bade also compensation to be made, again
   in gold,
For the men whom Grendel had horribly murdered.

What a banquet then was! Gladness mounted,
Bench-mirth rang, the bearers poured out wine
   from wonderful vessels.   Lēoð wæs āsungen,
Glēomannes gyd. Gamen eft āstāh,
Beorhtode bencswēg, byrelas sealdon
Wīn of wunderfatum.
When the evening came
They cleared away the benches, covered the floor
With beds and bolsters, the Geats placing by their heads
Their polished shields, the lindens of battle –
Always ready for war: what a nation they were!

Then they sank into sleep.
But it was soon made clear a survivor was still living.
Another foe grieving, ailing for its loss.
Ides āglǣcwīf yrmþe gemunde,
Sē þe wæteregesan wunian scolde,
Cealde strēamas, siþðan Cāin wearð
Tō ecgbanan āngan brēþer,
    fæderenmǣge;
In the chilling currents, dwelling in dread waters,
The monstrous ogress – Grendel's Mother!

Part Two

Grendel's mother now purposed, blackhearted,
   gluttonous,
On a wrath-bearing visit of vengeance for her son.
Ond his mōdor þā gȳt
Gīfre ond galgmōd gegān wolde
Sorhfulne sīð, sunu dēoð wrecan.
She descended on Heorot, and fate swept on its wheel
When the mother of Grendel found her way among
   those men.
Many a hard sword from its rack among the benches
Was by firm hand lifted, the broad shield raised.
She was all eager to be out of the place
Now she was discovered, and escape with her life.
She caught a man quickly, the King's good friend
   Ashere,
Clutched him to herself and was away to the fen.
(Beowulf was not there: separate lodging was assigned

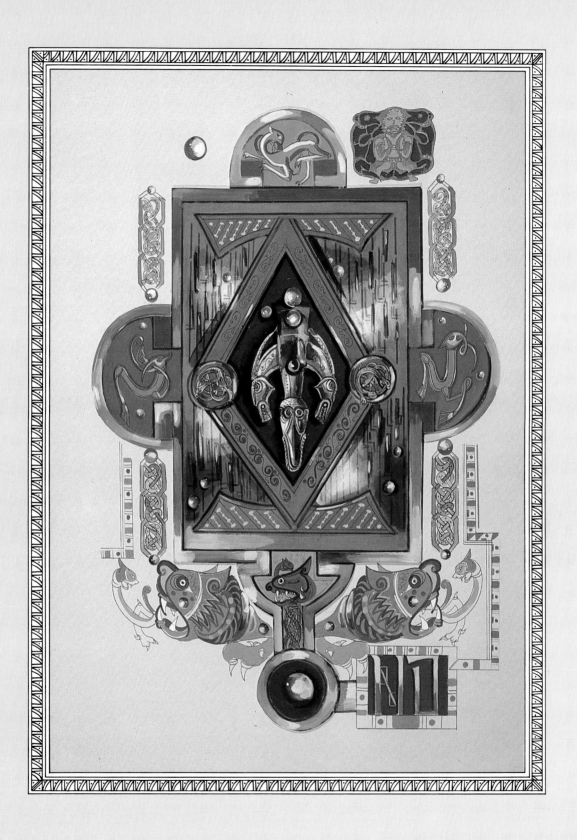

After the treasure-giving to the Geat champion).
Heorot was in uproar – Grendel's hand had gone
  with her!

Speedily Beowulf was summoned to the chamber.
The man excellent in warfare walked across the hall
Flanked by his escort – the floor-timbers boomed!
– To make his address to the Danish King,
And asked of him whether the night had been pleasant
After call so urgent: 'Do not ask about pleasure!
    Sorrow has returned
To the House of Denmark, with the death of Ashere,
My closest counsellor, keeper of my thoughts,
Strongest of warriors, famed in battle:
All men of birth and merit should be as Ashere.
A bloodthirsty monster has murdered him in Heorot.
Glorying in her carrion. She has taken vengeance
For the previous night – revenge is her motive.
I have heard it said by those who live in the country
That they have seen a pair of huge moor-haunters
Otherwordly ones: they know the man of old
By the name of Grendel and know of no father!
But this one's in woman's shape.

Mysterious is their region: wolf-fells, wind-picked moors,
A torrent of water falls from a lowering bluff
To an underground flood. Not far from here
The Mere lies, dark, overhung with hoar-frost.
A fire in the water!
The hart that roams the heath when the hounds have
    pressed him
May hide in the forest his antlered head:
But the hart will die there, sell his life on the brink
Rather than swim. Unholy that place is,
And the wind stirs up vile storms there, whipping
    swirling waters
Which climb to the clouds and make the skies weep.
Our sole remedy is to turn again to you.'

Beowulf spoke, son of Edgetheow: 'Bear your grief, wise one!
We must all expect to leave our life upon this earth,
But must earn some renown if we can, before death,
As did your friend Ashere.
Daring is the epitaph for every fighting man;
   þæt bið drihtguman
Unlifgendum æfter sēlest.
We shall rapidly find where this Grendel's mother's gone!

The old king leapt up and offered thanks to God,
To the Lord Almighty for what this man had spoken.
Steeds with braided manes were bridled then;
The hero and the monarch rode out shining together
And a troop of shield-bearers marched at their side.

The trace of her going, the track across the plain
Was clearly to be seen on the fog-bound moor,
The way she had carried the lifeless body, flailing,
Of the man who meant most to Hrothgar
   the Great King.
Reconnoitring ahead, Beowulf saw some ash-trees
Hung above a hoary rock, beneath which the water
Was turbid with blood, with warm upwellings:
And there they found, boiling with crimson,
The head of Ashhere by the edge of the cliff.

Then the war-horn sang, an eager battle-cry,
And Beowulf put on, unanxious for his life,
The mailed shirt – bulwark to his bone-framed chest –
A silver helmet – to strike down through swirl of water,
And the hilted sword which Hrothgar's spokesman
Unferth – yes, the taunter of the swimming match –

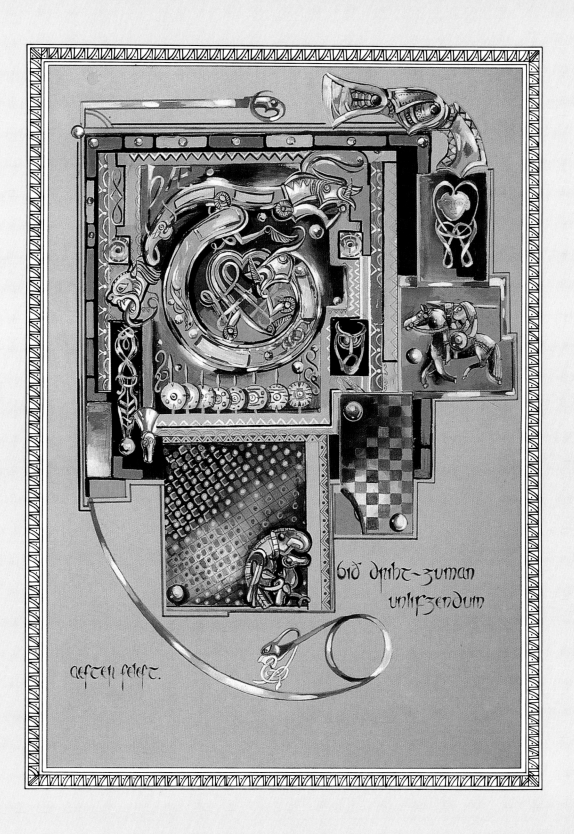

bid drihc-zuman
unlifzendum

aeften felet.

Had given him in this his hour of trial –
Its name, Hrunting, poison-twig patterned,
Never failing the hero whose hand took it up.
(It would seem that Unferth had forgotten
    his sarcasm
Spoken before when eloquent with wine!)
Then Beowulf spoke, son of Edgetheow:
'I am eager to begin, great son of Healfdene.
Remember your promise that if I should die
You will assume the place of father towards me:
And then let Unferth take back this blade
    he has given me –
He is widely known, and must not lose his glory!'
He then dived into the Mere not waiting for
    an answer:
And the surging water closed over his head.

He swam until noon before reaching the lake-floor.

The grim and greedy guardian of the flood
Keeping her hungry hundred-season watch,
Discovered at once that one from above,
A human, had sounded the home of the monsters.

She felt for the man, and fastened upon him
Her terrible hooks; but his mail-shirt so ringed him
She could not drive her fierce fingers
Through the mesh of that harness masking his limbs.
While she drew him, pinioned, down to her lair,
He could not draw his sword, for throngs
Of ripping tusks, sea beasts, attacked him.

Suddenly there was no water, he was in a vaulting chamber,
Saw a gleam and flashing, a bright fire blazing clear.
He then saw the size of this sea-demon woman.
He dashed out good Hrunting with such strength
   and violence
That the ring-banded sword screamed out
   loud on her head;
But the glittering metal refused to bite
Or hurt her at all: the edge had failed,
Though before in all conflicts it had carved through
   the helmet
Of each chosen man. Resolute again
Beowulf flung his sword to the ground,
Went for Grendel's mother,
Seized her by the shoulder, and with mounting anger
Swung the desperate enemy till she fell to the floor.

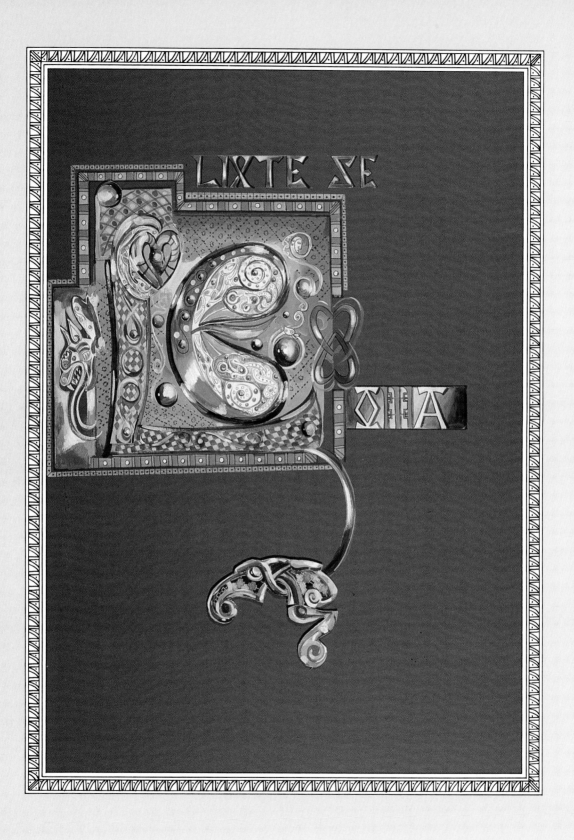

She promptly repaid this present of his
(Her boy was to be avenged, her only son)
Toppled his weariness, drew out her knife —
And had not the mail shirt o'erspreading his back
Well shielded his life, Edgetheow's son
Might have ended his venture neath vastness of earth.

Then he saw among the armour on the wall
A Giant-sword from former days.
This wonder was so enormous that no other man
Would be equal to bearing it in battle-play —
It was a Giant's forge that had fashioned it so well.
The Geat champion, shaking now with war-rage,
Caught it by the rich hilt and careless of his life
Brandished its circles and brought it down in fury
To take her full and fairly biting into the neck;
The blade sheared through the backbone.
She fell to the ground;
The sword was gory;
he was glad at the deed!

Līxte se lēoma, lēoht inne stōd,
Efne swā of hefene hādre scīneð
   rodores candel.

Light glowed out and illumined the chamber
With a clearness such as the candle of heaven
Sheds in the sky. And Beowulf saw where Grendel,
Wasted from his wound at the battle at Heorot,
His body gaping, open, lay waiting for his death.
The hard-swung sword struck — the settlement was made.
    Hē him þæs lēan forgeald.

From above, Hrothgar's men descried soon enough
The water stirred turbid and marbling the surface.
They thought it unlikely they'd see once again
The prince return triumphant to seek their famous master.
Surely the she-wolf had done away with him.
The ninth hour had come, so the keen-hearted Scyldings
Abandoned the cliff-head home-bound with their king.
But the Geats sat on, and stared at the pool,
Despairing to ever see Beowulf again.

The blood it had shed now made the giant sword dwindle.
Melt as the ice when spring's frost's grip unfastens;
Grendel's mother's hot blood had melted, burnt it,
So venomous the hell-fiend that died in that hall.

Then the Geat champion taking only that hilt
Bristling with jewels, the sword Hrunting, and Grendel's
  vile head,
Struck up through the water, through the rough wave-swirl,
Came strongly to land, where the watchers there, waiting,
Huge in relief,
Quickly loosened his helmet and shirt of fine mail.
Then bold as kings, carefree of heart,
They carried the head — four to a spear,
Retracing their tracks to the gold-giving hall.
They presented the head, held up by the locks,
Manhandled in where the men were all drinking;
A hideous sight for the thanes — and their queen —
An awesome thing; they eyed it well!

Beowulf presented himself to King Hrothgar: 'Behold!
My trophies here Great Son of Healfdene.
Now I say you may sleep in Heorot free from care,
Both young men and guard, my lord of the Scyldings.'

Hrothgar gazed on the head and hilt, the hall silent.
'Beowulf, my friend, your name shall resound
Through the nations of earth that are furthest away.

It is granted your people you shall live to be comfort
And bulwark to your heroes. The noon of your strength
Shall last for a while now, but we know in little time
Flame, drowning, spear, or ugliness of age
Will conquer you finally, O bravest of warriors.
So it is with myself! But now join those here seated
And rejoice in your feast, O man clad in victory!'

Next day, the sunlight shaking out above the shadows,
Each Geatish atheling was eager to be home,
And Beowulf ordered the sword Hrunting be returned
To Unferth – accounting it formidable in fight,
Finding its edges true – ample was his spirit!
    þæt wæs mōdig secg.

The fighting men were armed up ready for the journey
And Beowulf said: 'We sailors come from far
Wish to say how keenly we desire to return
To our own Lord Hygelac. We were right royally treated.
And if ever on this earth I can earn of you
More of your love than I have so far done,

If ever neighbouring tribes intend your harm,
I'll bring you a grove of grey-tipped spears
If you are short of men. We find many friends here.'

Hrothgar thanked him, said: 'As I come to know
Your temper, friend Beowulf, the more it pleases me.
You have brought it about that both Sea-Geats and Spear-Danes
Shall share out peace;
Your people, I know, always open-hearted,
Are firm towards enemies and fast to their friends!'

Riding at anchor, the wave-skimmer stayed
For her owner and lord. The coastguard saw
The heroes depart as he had seen them come,
Graciously greeted them, rode down to meet them.
The soaring prow, high masted, moved out to divide
The deep waters, skimming, left Denmark behind;
Furled back the waves, foam-throated seafarer,
Planing till they sighted the headlands they knew.

The Geatish harbour-guard, ever scouring
In their look-out for these men,
Now moored the broad-ribbed boat in the sand;

No pounding breakers should drive away again
Those darling timbers!
News of Beowulf's return was brought to King Hygelac,
The floor cleared for his band by order of the king.
Carrying the mead-cup was Hareth's daughter
Presenting the wine-bowl to the hand of each Geat.

Hygelac then made courteous enquiry –
Curiosity burned to know the adventures of these men!
'I pled with you continually never to meet
With that murderous creature, but to let the North Danes
Themselves bring an end to their Grendel feud.'

Beowulf spoke: 'Gracious Hygelac, it has been spoken
     aloud
What battle occasion befell me and Grendel.
When heaven's jewel, day's glory, had glided from
     the world
The dire-dusk fiend came down to seek us out –
The crimson-toothed slayer would not leave that gold-hall
     empty-handed!
He groped out a greedy palm, I grasped it,
And, tale too long to tell,

That hand stayed behind in the hall of Heorot!
When the ensuing dusk came, quick upon its heels,
The mother of Grendel moved to her revenge.
She struck down a warrior, carried the body
To the mountain-torrent's depths, hideous embrace.
I found in the surges that grimmest of guardians:
After hand-to-hand struggle, the whirlpool boiled
With the blood of the mother – I'd slashed off her head
In that hall underground with a sword of huge size!
O, the great King Hrothgar rewarded me well
With a heap of treasures, all I desired,
Now, oh bravest of kings, I present them to you.'

Then Hygelac, responding, bid them bring in
The sword heirloom of Geatland, elaborate in gold,
Bid them place it in the lap of Beowulf, son of Edgetheow.
Also bestowed on him seven thousand hides,
A chief's stool, and hall –
Before, Beowulf's family, the house of Waymundings
Only held rank of sword; now inherited a birthright,
The greatest region of all the wide kingdom.

Part Three

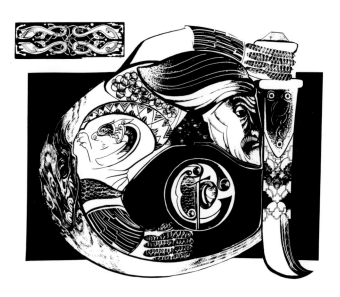

Now it fell out much later, when Hygelac died,
And despite the shield's shelter, his son Heardred
   was dead,
That the broad kingdom came by this turn
Into Beowulf's hands. Half a century he ruled it –
But where are you now my noblest treasure-sharer?
I cannot look upon these ruined walls
And not cry out, 'Where are they now?
The many matchless heroes, the proud horsemen
   and their steeds?
Where the feasting faces round this table?
Where is the gladness this grim hall once knew?'
Under these skies, Wyrd's *will alone endures:*
Here wealth is lent us, friends are lent us,
Heroes are mortal and kinsfolk pass away,
And here at last the Earth's wide frame itself
Shall come to desolation.

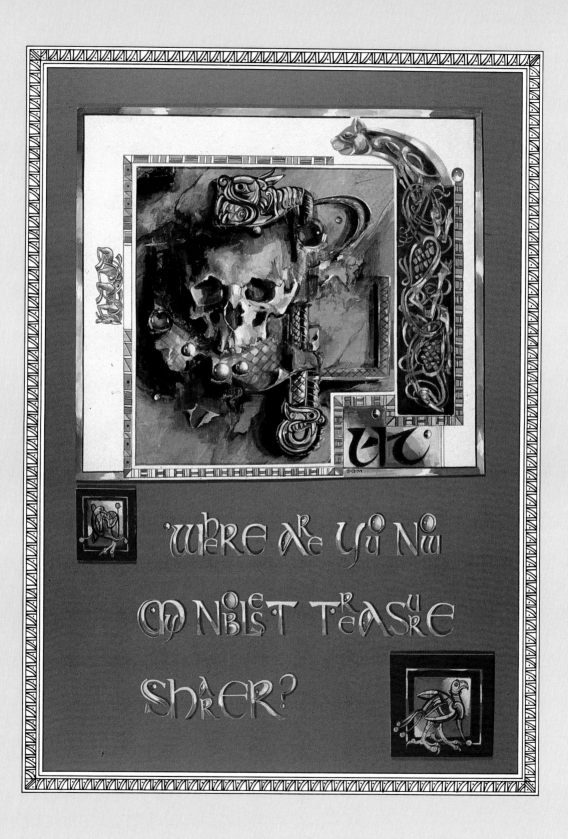

WHERE ARE YU NOW

MY NOBLST TREASURE

SHIER?

E ÞEREOLO

TELA
FICTIT
WINTRA

But Beowulf wæs ðā frōd cyning,
Hē gehēold tela fīftig wintra;
Fifty winters he ruled,
Grew grey in guardianship of the land
Till one began, a hoard-guarding dragon,
To put forth his power in the pitch-black night-times.
He guarded a gold-hoard in a towering stone
   burial-mound.
Men knew not its entrance, but one day a slave
On the run from a flogging felt his way in.
When he saw the dragon there he was struck
   with great terror,
But even so stole from thence a solid gold cup.

In another age an unknown man, heavy with friend-loss,
Had brought in and hid here his beloved gold hoard.
Saying: 'Hold ground, for men could not,
   the gold of the earls.
This hardened helmet, healed with gold
Shall lose its shell;
This cuirass, that in the crash took bite of iron
Will moulder with man.
This mail-shirt, hung from a shoulder that
   shouldered warriors, shall not jingle again.

There's no joy from harp-play,
No *hawk* swings through the hall now,
  no horse tramps the threshold;
Terrible slaughter has carried to darkness many
  kindreds of men.'

Then he left the stone barrow, and the smooth evil dragon,
Bound from of old to seek barrow hoards
And guard for all time the gold that he finds,
Swam through the gloom enfolded in flame.
And for three hundred winters this dragon-fiend, swooper,
Sleek-skinned by night, guarded the hoard-hall –
Till that slave woke his anger by bearing to his master
The golden goblet as a peace offering.

The dragon reptile woke, snuffed along the rock,
Circled in flames to discover the robber:
No *hint of man!* – But this meant war, pleased him.
He rejoiced at the thought of action in battle
And waited till evening only with difficulty –
His fire, he swore, would requite the lost cup!

Night falling, he issued out, belched glowing flakes,
He burnt the bright buildings: the blazing rose skyward
And men were afraid – the flying scourge
Did not mean to leave one living thing.
Before morning's light he flew back to his chamber,
He had lapped the people of the land in fire,
And trusted now to the barrow's strength.
His faith misled him! Him sēo wēn gelēah.

Beowulf knew soon enough the truth of the horror
For his own hall itself had been swallowed in flame.
Supposing he had angered the Eternal Lord,
His breast was thronged with unaccustomed, care-filled
   thoughts.
But this king of the Geats now planned a punishment,
Commanded the making of a shield all in iron,
Well knowing one of linden would fail him in fire.
He disdained to attack with a troop of men,
Having clashed with many since his cleansing of Heorot
And did not fear death.
He went with eleven to set eyes on the serpent,
Having by then discovered the cause of the outrage;

The precious drinking-cup had passed into his hands
From the hands of the finder — and that miserable slave
Now made the thirteenth man in their company.
Cowed, he must show them the way to the place,
For he alone knew the knoll and its earth-hall,
That underground hollow heaped with intricate treasures.

The war-seasoned king sat down on the headland,
Spoke encouraging words to the friends of his hearth:
But gloomy his spirit, death-eager, wandering;
He knew that fate waited to seek his soul's hoard.
   Him wæs geōmor sefa,
Wǣfre ond wælfūs, wyrd ungemete nēah,
Sē ðone gomelan grētan sceolde,
Sēcean sāwle hord.

Beowulf spoke long, recalling past conflicts,
Then ended his discourse with open-heart boast!
'Battles in plenty I ventured in youth,
And old as I am now I'll again achieve glory
If this evil destroyer once dares venture forth.
I would take no sword, no weapon to the serpent,
If I knew another way to fight him — as with Grendel before;

But as I must expect hot war-breath and venom,
I shall take the precautions of chain-mail and shield.
My mood is strong! Men in armour, wait here on the barrow.
It's my fate alone to match strength with this worm,
Win the treasure by daring or die in the fight.'

The champion stood up and bore his shield
To the rocky cliff's foot; saw in the wall
An archway of stone and a stream there breaking
From the burial barrow – a stream of fire,
A boiling watercourse of killing flames.
Filled with rage, Beowulf uttered a shout from his breast;
His voice re-echoed through the vault of grey-stone;
The treasure-guardian heard, billowed out from the rock
In a hissing gust – the grey ground boomed!
Beowulf flung up his shield, shook out his sharp sword;
Each of the pair, intending destruction, was horror
    to the other.

The fleetness of the serpent wound itself together,
Came flowing forward, flaming and coiling.
Our chief raised his hand and brought down such a stroke

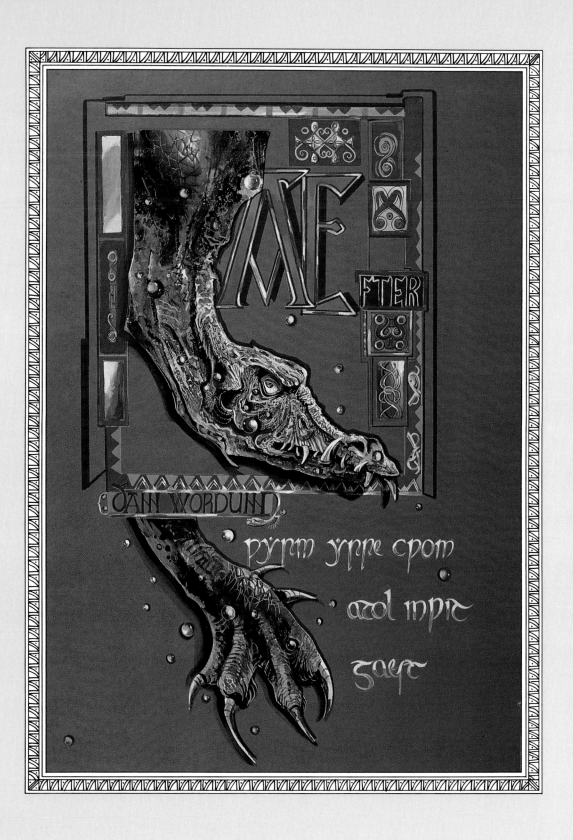

With his ancestral sword that, meeting the bone,
It turned, bit less strongly than required of it then;
The bared battle-blade had failed in the fight!
After this cut the worm grew savage-minded!
Spat death-fire, war flashes blazed in the distance,
Fire fenced in the folk-king: he felt bitter pain.

His band of companions did not stand about him
As battle usage asks, but fled to the forest
And looked after their lives.
All but one, his name Wiglaf, Son of Weoxstan,
Geatish prince of Beowulf's house of the Waymundings.
His liege-lord he saw, tormented by heat,
And remembering the favours formally given him
Restoring the landrights his father had held,
He could not hold back, seized yellow shield of linden,
Drew ancient sword. His courage was firm,
As the serpent soon found when they came there to grips.
He strode through the blood-smoke, bore his war helmet
To the aid of his lord: 'Beloved Beowulf, bear all well!
You gave out in your youth you would never allow
Your glory to abate; defend your life now
With your utmost of strength — my help shall be yours.'

Hearing these words, the dragon came raging,
Attacked once again, terror-fire flashing.
Wiglaf's mail did not serve, and his shield was withered
Back to the boss in the billow of fire.
But nothing deterred, the young man dodged back,
Stepped smartly to take up his kinsman's protection.
And then did that king remember his worth,
Dealt out a sword-blow of annihilating weight,
Striking into the head; but the hero's sword shattered,
His hand was so strong. (I have heard any sword
He bore into battle, his blow would o'ertax –
So it happened with this). Now a third time the fire-drake,
His chance lying open, rushed in on our king,
Crushed all his neck between bitter fangs.
Wiglaf then, disregarding the head, struck below it,
Aimed true, and the fire quickly slackened in consequence.
Then Beowulf, recovering, reached for his stabbing-knife,
Hewed mightily down – hacked the dragon in half!

So daring drove out life; ferh ellen wræc;
And the king saw the last triumph of his works in the world.

His wound burned and swelled, the bane boiled in his chest,
The poison within him. He walked away thinking,
Sat down on a ledge and surveyed the old earth-hall.
Wiglaf took water and washed his good lord.
Bathed away battle blood, loosened his helmet.

The king spoke through his pain: 'I would now wish
    my war-gear
Be given my son, if such heir, flesh of flesh,
Had been granted to me. I have guarded this people
For full half a century, and there wasn't a king
Dared afront me with war; I held my own well,
Seldom swore wrongful oaths! In all of these things
I may still rejoice. Quickly go now Good Wiglaf
And look on the hoard: make haste that I may gaze
On that golden inheritance, the clear skilful jewels;
So that I by that treasury may be more assuaged,
Leaving the life and the lordship that I have long held.

Straightway, the son of Weoxstan obeyed his
    wounded lord,
Entered the barrow – was thrilled at the sight

Of gold in its glitter littering the ground.
He hurried back to Beowulf, eager to return,
Bearing some of the treasures: came upon his King
Covered in blood and at his life's end. 'I wish to
      thank my God for these treasures I see,
For making me able to win for my people
Such a trophy as this. You, Wiglaf, must attend
To the people's need henceforth, no further may I stay;
Bid men build me a tomb on the foreland by the sea,
That shall stand as reminder of me to my folk,
Towering high above Hronesness;
So that ocean travellers shall afterwards name it
      "Beowulf's Barrow",
Bending in the distance through the mists upon the sea.'
He unclasped his golden collar, harness and arm-ring,
Gold-plated helmet, gave to the young warrior,
Bēah ond byrnan, *his crown and coat of mail,*
Hēt hyne brūcan well
Bade him use them well:
'You are the last of our house of the Waymundings!
My people are gone, and I must them follow.'
These his last words ere his soul left his breast,
Mounting to meet with the glory of the righteous.

It was soon after this that the ten battle-shirkers,
All traitors and weaklings, came out of the wood.
They bore their shields ashamedly to where
   the old man lay,
Wiglaf trying to revive him, without any success.
'Companions of the guard!
Your kinsmen shall become wanderers without land-rights
As soon as athelings over the world
Shall hear how you fled. But haste is best now:
We must bear our ring-bestower on his road.
Let the owners of homesteads and all worthy warriors
From far and wide fetch in wood for the hero's funeral pyre.
Nobody shall wear an arm-ring in his memory:
No maiden's neck be enhanced by bearing these rings.
Bereft of gold rather.
Many a spear shall henceforth feel cold in the mornings
Nor shall the harper's melody arouse them for fight.'

They entered the gold chamber and soon carried out
The precious treasures; pushed the dragon over the cliff,
Let the waves take him and the flood him engulf.
The untold profusion of twisted gold
Was loaded on a wagon, and the warrior prince
Borne hoary-headed to Hronesness.

The Geat race then reared up a funeral pyre –
Shining mail and shields of war and helmets hung upon it –
They laid out in the middle the body of their chief,
And on top there then kindled the biggest funeral fire.
The roaring of flames mingled with weeping
As the fire's red heart consumed the house of bone.
Heaven swallowed the smoke.

Then in only ten days Beowulf's followers constructed
A fortress on the headland, a beacon high and broad.
What remained of the fire they cast a wall around,
placed in the tomb both the torques and the jewels,
And they dwell there yet, of no more use to man
Than in ages before!

Then they rode around the barrow, twelve in all,
    atheling's sons,
Reciting their dirge to declare their grief:
They praised their king's manhood and the prowess
    of his hands;
They raised his name; it is right a man
Be lavish in honouring his lord and his friend,
Should love him in his heart, when the leading-forth
From the house of flesh befalls him at last.

This was the manner of the mourning of the Geats,
Sharers in the feast, at the fall of their lord;
They said he had proved of all kings in the world
The gentlest of men, the most gracious,
The kindest to his people, the keenest for fame.

Cwǣdon þæt hē wǣre wyruldcyninga
Manna mildust ond monðwǣrust,
Lēodum līðost ond lofgeornost.

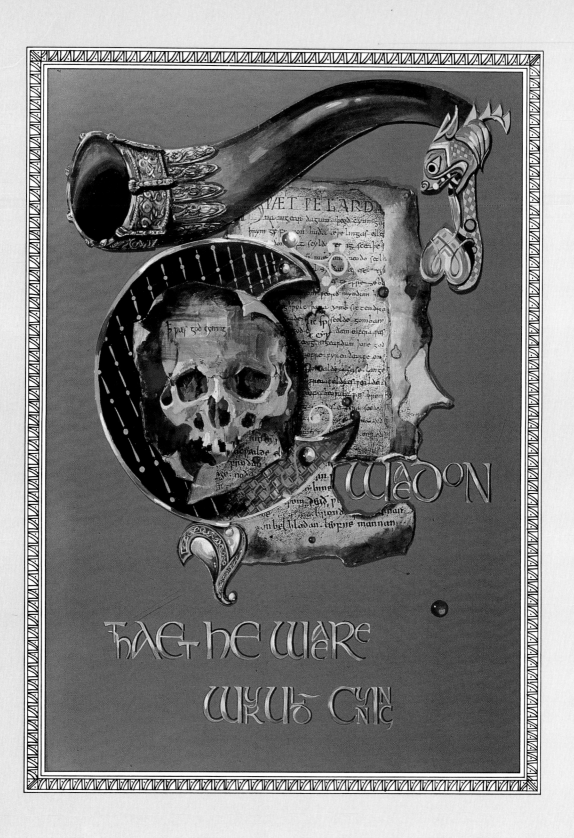

þæs
god cƿning.